Nana's
Treasured Recipes

for my granddaughter

www.FromtheRookery.com

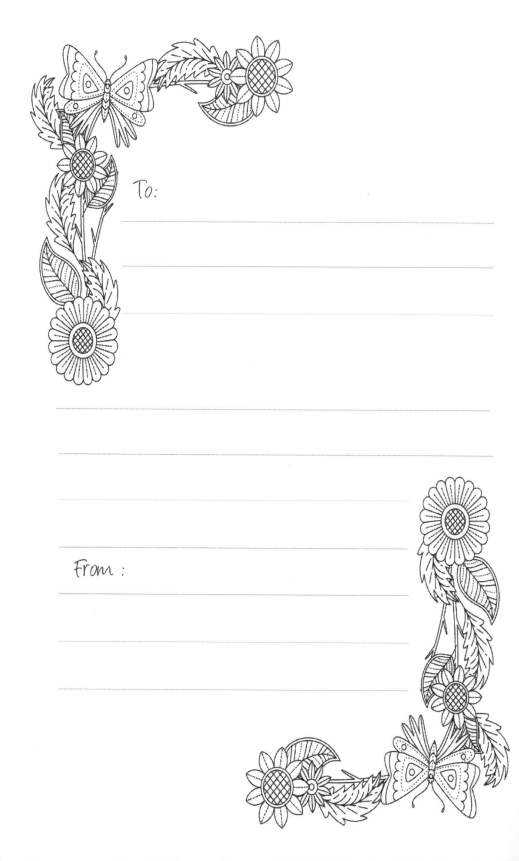

To:

From :

These recipes are handed down from
me to you with love.
They have served me well and I hope
they do the same with you.
They are carefullly handwritten so a
part of me is contained within the
pages – alongside my happy memories
of eating good food with friends and
family – and my wishes of the same
for you.
Some of the recipe pages have been
left blank and I hope in the future
you add the recipes that you discover
and love. Perhaps one day the
book will be passed on, with both our
good wishes, to someone you cherish too.

XX

Food preparation and storage tips

Kitchen tips and techniques

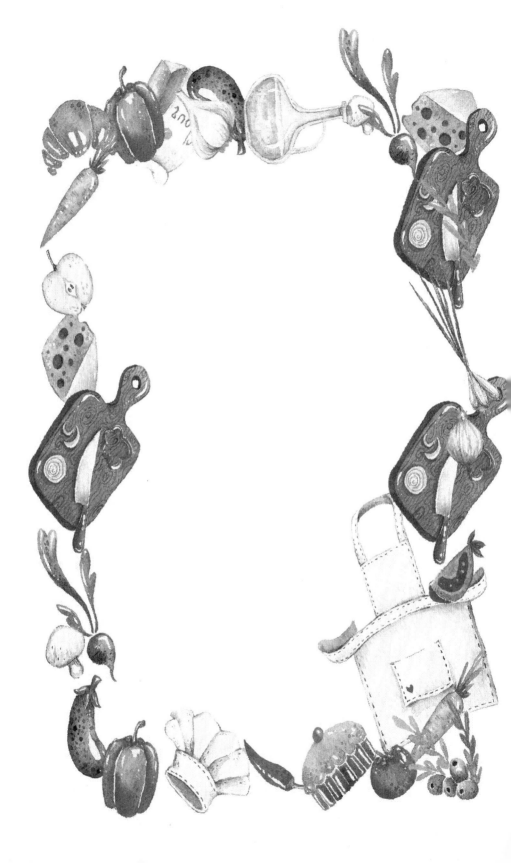

Recipes

Recipe

_____
_____
_____
_____
_____

Serves _____

Time to make _____

Oven Temp. _____
_____

Ingredients

_____
_____
_____
_____
_____
_____
_____
_____
_____
_____
_____

Instructions

Recipe

_____
_____
_____
_____
_____

Serves _____

Time to make _____

Oven Temp. _____
_____

Ingredients

_____
_____
_____
_____
_____
_____
_____
_____
_____
_____

Instructions

Recipe

_____
_____
_____
_____
_____

Serves
_____

Time to make
_____

Oven Temp.
_____

Ingredients

_____
_____
_____
_____
_____
_____
_____
_____
_____
_____
_____

Instructions

Recipe

_____
_____
_____
_____
_____

Serves
_____

Time to make
_____

Oven Temp.
_____

Ingredients

_____
_____
_____
_____
_____
_____
_____
_____
_____
_____
_____

Instructions

Recipe

_____
_____
_____
_____
_____

Serves
_____

Time to make
_____

Oven Temp.
_____

Ingredients

_____
_____
_____
_____
_____
_____
_____
_____
_____
_____
_____

Instructions

Recipe

_____
_____
_____
_____
_____

Serves
_____

Time to make
_____

Oven Temp.
_____

Ingredients

_____
_____
_____
_____
_____
_____
_____
_____
_____
_____
_____
_____

Instructions

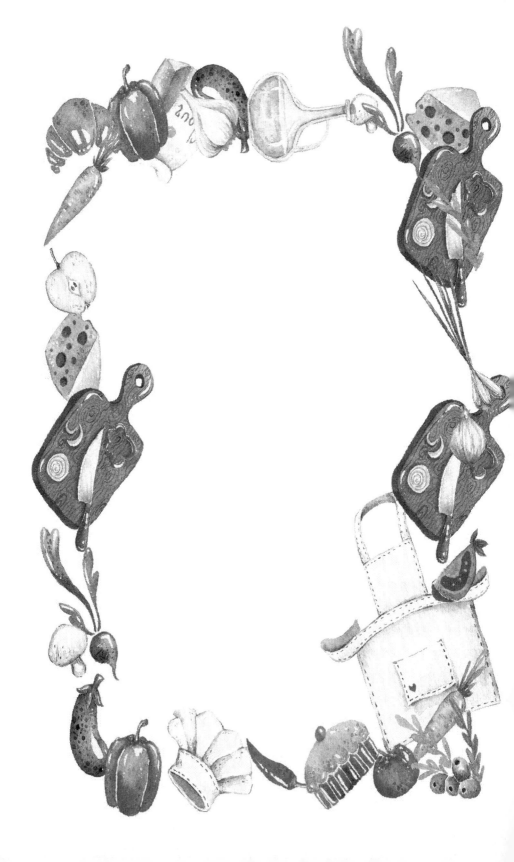

Recipes

Recipe

_____

_____

_____

_____

_____

Serves _____

Time to make _____

Oven Temp. _____

_____

Ingredients

_____

_____

_____

_____

_____

_____

_____

_____

_____

_____

_____

_____

_____

Instructions

Recipe

_____
_____
_____
_____
_____

Serves
_____

Time to make
_____

Oven Temp.
_____

Ingredients

_____
_____
_____
_____
_____
_____
_____
_____
_____
_____
_____

Instructions

Recipe

_____
_____
_____
_____
_____

Serves _____

Time to make _____

Oven Temp. _____

_____

Ingredients

_____
_____
_____
_____
_____
_____
_____
_____
_____
_____
_____

Instructions

Recipe

_____
_____
_____
_____

Serves _____

Time to make _____

Oven Temp. _____

_____

Ingredients

_____
_____
_____
_____
_____
_____
_____
_____
_____
_____
_____
_____
_____

Instructions

Recipe

_____
_____
_____
_____
_____

Serves _____

Time to make _____

Oven Temp. _____
_____

Ingredients

_____
_____
_____
_____
_____
_____
_____
_____
_____
_____
_____
_____
_____

Instructions

Recipe

_____
_____
_____
_____
_____

Serves _____

Time to make _____

Oven Temp. _____
_____

Ingredients

_____
_____
_____
_____
_____
_____
_____
_____
_____
_____
_____
_____
_____

Instructions

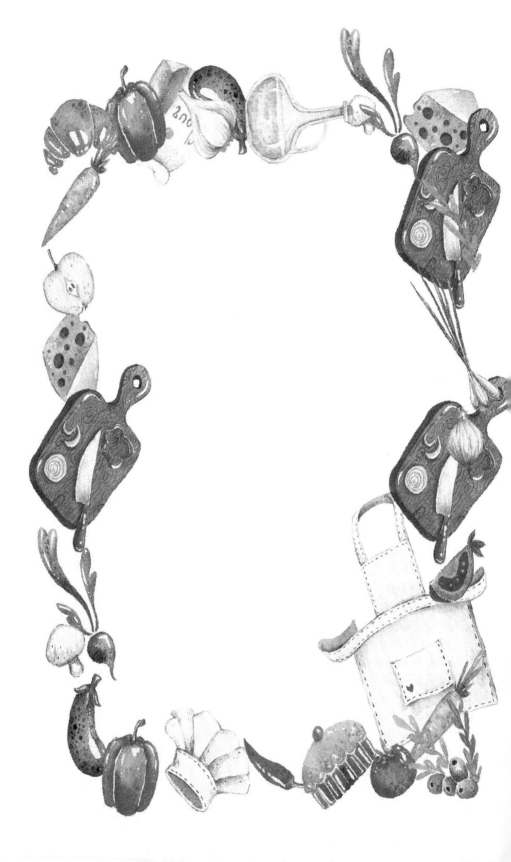

....

....

....

Recipes

Recipe

_____
_____
_____
_____
_____

Serves _____

Time to make _____

Oven Temp. _____
_____

Ingredients

_____
_____
_____
_____
_____
_____
_____
_____
_____
_____
_____
_____

Instructions

Recipe

Serves

Time to make

Oven Temp.

Ingredients

Instructions

Recipe

_____
_____
_____
_____
_____

Serves _____

Time to make _____

Oven Temp. _____
_____

Ingredients

_____
_____
_____
_____
_____
_____
_____
_____
_____
_____
_____
_____
_____

Instructions

Recipe

Serves

Time to make

Oven Temp.

Ingredients

Instructions

Recipe

_____
_____
_____
_____
_____

Serves
_____

Time to make
_____

Oven Temp.
_____

Ingredients

_____
_____
_____
_____
_____
_____
_____
_____
_____
_____
_____
_____

Instructions

Recipe

Serves

Time to make

Oven Temp.

Ingredients

Instructions

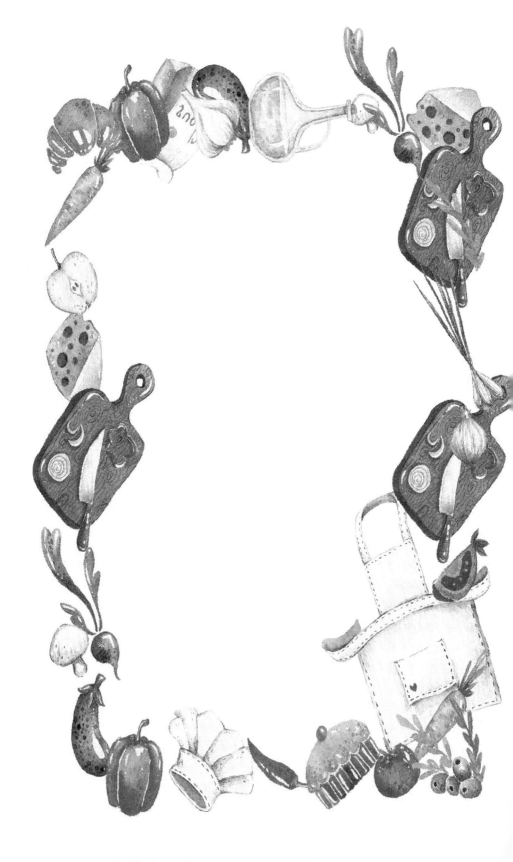

Recipes

Recipe

_____
_____
_____
_____
_____

Serves
_____

Time to make
_____

Oven Temp.
_____

Ingredients

_____
_____
_____
_____
_____
_____
_____
_____
_____
_____
_____

Instructions

Recipe

Serves

Time to make

Oven Temp.

Ingredients

Instructions

Recipe

_____
_____
_____
_____
_____

Serves _____

Time to make _____

Oven Temp. _____
_____

Ingredients

_____
_____
_____
_____
_____
_____
_____
_____
_____
_____
_____
_____
_____

Instructions

Recipe

Serves

Time to make

Oven Temp.

Ingredients

Instructions

Recipe

_____
_____
_____
_____
_____

Serves
_____

Time to make
_____

Oven Temp.
_____

Ingredients

_____
_____
_____
_____
_____
_____
_____
_____
_____
_____
_____
_____

Instructions

Recipe

Serves

Time to make

Oven Temp.

Ingredients

Instructions

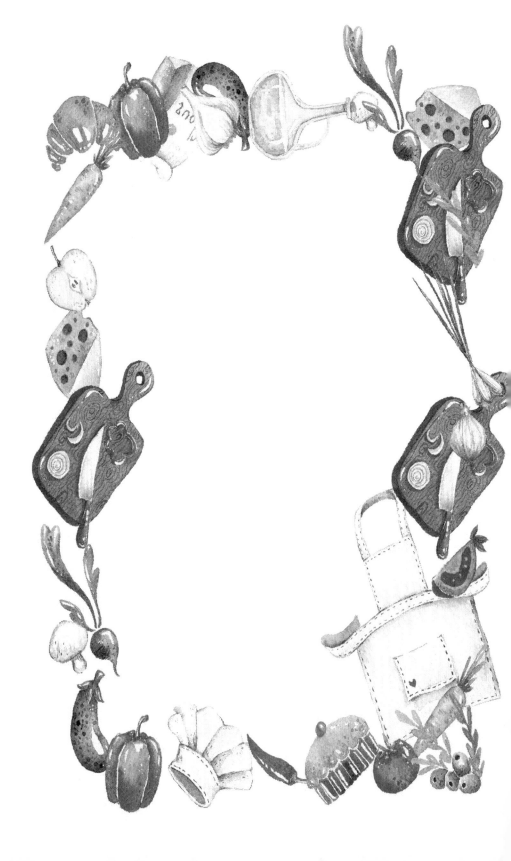

Recipes

Recipe

_____

_____

_____

_____

_____

Serves _____

Time to make _____

Oven Temp. _____

_____

Ingredients

_____

_____

_____

_____

_____

_____

_____

_____

_____

_____

_____

_____

Instructions

Recipe

_____
_____
_____
_____
_____

Serves _____

Time to make _____

Oven Temp. _____
_____

Ingredients

_____
_____
_____
_____
_____
_____
_____
_____
_____
_____
_____
_____
_____

Instructions

Recipe

_____
_____
_____
_____
_____

Serves _____

Time to make _____

Oven Temp. _____
_____

Ingredients

_____
_____
_____
_____
_____
_____
_____
_____
_____
_____
_____
_____

Instructions

Recipe

_____
_____
_____
_____
_____

Serves _____

Time to make _____

Oven Temp. _____
_____

Ingredients

_____
_____
_____
_____
_____
_____
_____
_____
_____
_____
_____

Instructions

Recipe

_____
_____
_____
_____
_____

Serves _____

Time to make _____

Oven Temp. _____
_____

Ingredients

_____
_____
_____
_____
_____
_____
_____
_____
_____
_____
_____
_____

Instructions

Recipe

_____
_____
_____
_____
_____

Serves _____

Time to make _____

Oven Temp. _____
_____

Ingredients

_____
_____
_____
_____
_____
_____
_____
_____
_____
_____
_____

Instructions

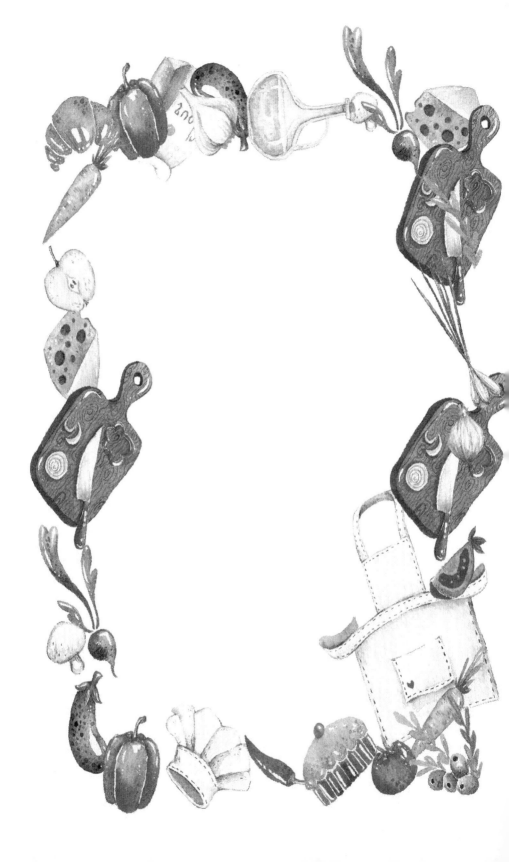

Recipes

Recipe

_____
_____
_____
_____
_____

Serves _____

Time to make _____

Oven Temp. _____
_____

Ingredients

_____
_____
_____
_____
_____
_____
_____
_____
_____
_____
_____
_____

Recipe

_____
_____
_____
_____
_____

Serves _____

Time to make _____

Oven Temp. _____
_____

Ingredients

_____
_____
_____
_____
_____
_____
_____
_____
_____
_____
_____

Recipe

Serves

Time to make

Oven Temp.

Ingredients

Recipe

_____
_____
_____
_____
_____

Serves _____

Time to make _____

Oven Temp. _____
_____

Ingredients

_____
_____
_____
_____
_____
_____
_____
_____
_____
_____
_____
_____

Recipe

_____
_____
_____
_____
_____

Serves _____

Time to make _____

Oven Temp. _____
_____

Ingredients

_____
_____
_____
_____
_____
_____
_____
_____
_____
_____
_____

Recipe

_____
_____
_____
_____
_____

Serves _____

Time to make _____

Oven Temp. _____
_____

Ingredients

_____
_____
_____
_____
_____
_____
_____
_____
_____
_____
_____
_____

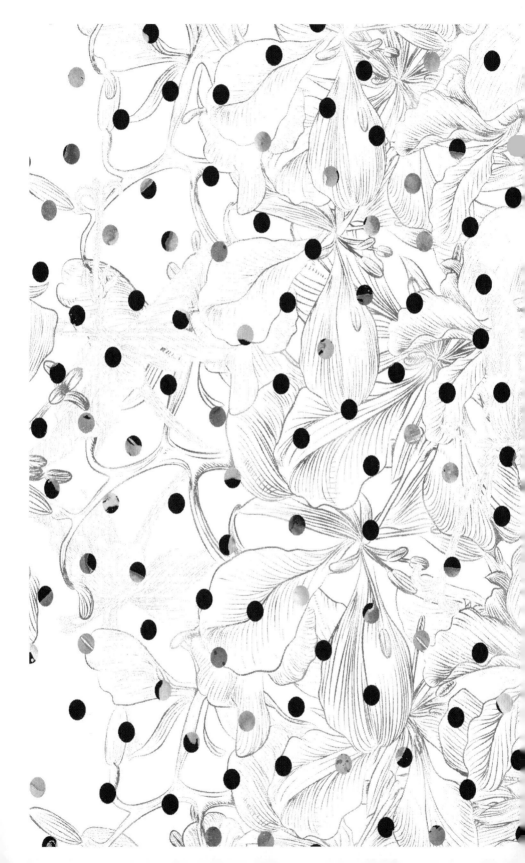

Happy food memories...

Happy cooking memories...

Notes:

Notes:

Instead of:	Amount	Use:
Arborio rice	1 cup	1 cup uncooked short-grain white rice, regular long-grain rice or brown rice
Baking powder	1 tsp	1/4 tsp baking soda plus 1/2 tsp cream of tartar
Balsamic vinegar	1 Tbsp	1 Tbsp sherry or cider vinegar
Beer	1 cup	1 cup non-alcoholic beer, apple cider or beef broth
Bread crumbs, dry	1/4 cup	1/4 cup finely crushed cracker crumbs, corn flakes or quick-cooking or old-fashioned oats
Broth, chicken, beef or vegetable	1 cup	1 tsp chicken, beef or vegetable bouillon granules (or 1 cube) dissolved in 1 cup boiling water
Brown sugar, packed	1 cup	1 cup granulated sugar mixed with 2 Tbsp molasses or dark corn syrup
Buttermilk or sour milk	1 cup	1 Tbsp lemon juice or white vinegar plus enough milk to make 1 cup; let stand a few minutes. Or 1 cup plain yogurt.
Chocolate Semisweet baking Semisweet chips Unsweetened baking	1 oz 1 cup 1 oz	1 oz unsweetened baking chocolate plus 1 Tbsp sugar 6 oz semisweet baking chocolate, chopped 3 Tbsp baking cocoa plus 1 Tbsp vegetable oil or melted shortening or margarine
Corn starch	1 Tbsp	2 Tbsp all-purpose flour or 4 tsp quick-cooking tapioca
Corn syrup Light Dark	1 cup 1 cup	1 cup granulated sugar plus 1/4 cup water 1 cup light corn syrup; 3/4 cup light corn syrup plus 1/4 cup molasses; 1 cup maple-flavored syrup
Eggs	1 large	2 egg whites; 1/4 cup fat-free cholesterol-free egg product; 2 egg yolks (for custard or puddings); or 2 egg yolks plus 1 Tbsp water (for cookies or bars)
Flour All-purpose Cake Self-rising	1 cup 1 cup 1 cup	1 cup plus 2 Tbsp cake flour 1 cup minus 2 Tbsp all-purpose flour 1 cup all-purpose flour plus 1 1/2 tsp baking powder and 1/2 tsp salt
Garlic, finely chopped	1	1/8 tsp garlic powder or 1/4 tsp instant minced garlic
Gingerroot, grated or finely chopped	1 tsp	3/4 tsp ground ginger
Herbs, chopped fresh	1 Tbsp	3/4 to 1 tsp dried herbs
Lemon juice, fresh	1 Tbsp	1 Tbsp bottled lemon juice or white vinegar
Lemon peel, grated	1 tsp	1 tsp dried lemon peel
Milk, regular or low-fat	1 cup	1/2 cup evaporated milk plus 1/2 cup water; or nonfat dry milk prepared as directed on package
Mushrooms, fresh	1 cup	1 can (4 oz) mushroom pieces and stems, drained
Mustard, yellow	1 Tbsp	1 tsp ground mustard
Poultry seasoning	1 tsp	1/4 tsp ground thyme plus 3/4 tsp ground sage
Pumpkin or apple pie spice	1 tsp	Mix 1/2 tsp ground cinnamon, 1/4 tsp ground ginger, 1/8 tsp ground allspice and 1/8 tsp ground nutmeg.
Sour cream	1 cup	1 cup plain yogurt
Tomato juice	1 cup	1/2 cup tomato sauce plus 1/2 cup water
Tomato paste	1/2 cup	1 cup tomato sauce cooked uncovered to reduce to 1/2 cup
Tomato sauce	2 cups	3/4 cup tomato paste plus 1 cup water
Tomatoes, canned	1 cup	About 1 1/3 cups cut-up fresh tomatoes, simmered 10 min
Wine, Red White	1 cup 1 cup	1 cup nonalcoholic wine, apple cider, beef broth, tomato juice or water 1 cup nonalcoholic wine, white grape juice, apple juice, chicken broth or water
Yeast, regular or quick active dry	1 pkg (1/4 oz)	2 1/4 tsp regular or quick active dry or 1 package (0.6 oz) compressed cake yeast
Yogurt, plain	1 cup	1 cup sour cream

Made in the USA
Las Vegas, NV
27 October 2021